HORSE BREEDS

CLYDESDALE

BY WHITNEY SANDERSON

Kids Core
An Imprint of Abdo Publishing
abdobooks.com

abdobooks.com

Published by Abdo Publishing, a division of ABDO, PO Box 398166, Minneapolis, Minnesota 55439. Copyright © 2026 by Abdo Consulting Group, Inc. International copyrights reserved in all countries. No part of this book may be reproduced in any form without written permission from the publisher. Kids Core™ is a trademark and logo of Abdo Publishing.

Printed in the United States of America, North Mankato, Minnesota.
052025
092025

Cover Photo: Shutterstock Images
Interior Photos: David Bagnall/Alamy, 4–5; Tim Gainey/Alamy, 6; Maurice McDonald/PA Images/Getty Images, 7; Shutterstock Images, 9, 18–19, 22, 28–29; Sanka Vidanagama/NurPhoto/Getty Images, 10; Universal History Archive/Universal Images Group/Getty Images, 12–13; Stephen Barnes/Farming/Alamy, 14; Mark J. Barrett/Alamy, 16; Andrew Milligan/WPA Pool/Getty Images Entertainment/Getty Images, 21; John Bracegirdle/Alamy, 25; Findlay/Alamy Live News/Alamy, 26

Editor: Marie Pearson
Series Designer: Ryan Gale

Library of Congress Control Number: 2024949004

Publisher's Cataloging-in-Publication Data

Names: Sanderson, Whitney, author.
Title: Clydesdale / by Whitney Sanderson
Description: Minneapolis, Minnesota: Abdo Publishing, 2026 | Series: Horse breeds | Includes online resources and index.
Identifiers: ISBN 9781098297503 (lib. bdg.) | ISBN 9798384930020 (ebook)
Subjects: LCSH: Clydesdale horse--Juvenile literature. | Horses--Juvenile literature. | Horse breeds--Juvenile literature. | Zoology--Juvenile literature.
Classification: DDC 636.15--dc23

CONTENTS

Clydesdales do not need roads to pull logs in forests.

CHAPTER 1

HORSEPOWER

Alex walked through the woods with his Clydesdale, Luna. He spotted a tree that was ready to be cut down. Alex used his chainsaw to cut down the tree. Luna stood patiently out of the way.

It takes a lot of training before a Clydesdale is ready to work.

A loop of chain hung from the back of a two-wheeled **logging arch**. After cutting the log, Alex wrapped the chain around it. “Get up, Luna!” Alex said cheerfully. He made a clucking sound. Luna leaned into the harness and pulled. The log began to slide across the forest floor.

Alex walked behind and a little to the right of Luna. He guided her with a set of long reins attached to her harness. He also used his voice.

Horses are much lighter than the machines used in logging, so they do less damage to the environment.

Luna skidded, or pulled, the log between the trees. Unlike heavy logging machines, Luna could work in the forest without causing much damage.

They skidded the log to a clearing near the road. A forklift driver would load it onto a truck headed to the sawmill. By sunset, Alex and Luna had hauled a big pile of timber. Alex was tired. But he felt good about the work he and Luna had done that day.

Feeding a Clydesdale

A full-grown Clydesdale eats up to 60 pounds (30 kg) of hay per day. This horse also eats about 20 pounds (9 kg) of grain each day. It drinks 30 gallons (110 L) of water. Clydesdales also produce a lot of manure, or poop. The manure can help farmers. Dried horse manure makes great **fertilizer**!

Each horse in a team must have a similar size and build so they move at the same speed.

Working Horses

The Clydesdale is a breed of draft horse. Drafts are strong horses that were bred to pull heavy loads. Clydesdales are famous for their size and power. In 2018 at the Iowa State Fair, a team of two Clydesdales pulled 13,500 pounds (6,120 kg). That is as heavy as two large pickup trucks!

Some zoos keep Clydesdales in their farm animal sections.

There are about 5,000 Clydesdales living today, making it a rare breed. Clydesdales have calm and friendly personalities. They are often called gentle giants.

Equiculture is a draft horse **sanctuary** and working farm in Maine. Several of its horses are Clydesdales. The farm's website says about the breed:

> They are known for their calm temperament and [are] not spooked very easily. This makes them great for high-stress environments and [is] why you see them in cities and parades.

Source: "Blue." *Equiculture*, n.d., equiculture.online. Accessed 15 Jan. 2025.

Comparing Texts

Think about the quote. Does it support the information in the chapter? Or does it give a different perspective? Explain how in a few sentences.

A painting from the mid-1700s shows two Clydesdales harnessed to a plow.

HISTORY OF THE CLYDESDALE

The Clydesdale breed began in the 1700s in Lanarkshire, Scotland. The River Clyde flowed nearby. Farmers who lived there bred their horses with bigger, stronger horses from England, Belgium, and the Netherlands.

The plows Clydesdales pull loosen the soil so seeds can be planted.

Some of the **ancestors** of these horses were war horses used by knights in the Middle Ages (500–1500 CE).

Clydesdale horses became famous for their strength. They plowed soil in fields and helped people plant crops. They hauled loads of coal from mines to cities.

Clydesdales were first brought to North America in the 1840s. They and other draft horses played a big role in building the first railroads in many countries. They hauled heavy building materials and carried away rocks and rubble.

Braids

Clydesdales in harnesses often have their manes and tails braided. This helps keep the hair from tangling in the harness. In shows, colorful ribbons are often used in the braids. People can add flights, which are colorful pieces that stick up from the mane. Braids with flights make the curve of the neck more noticeable.

Some people continue to breed Clydesdales today.

Saving the Clydesdale

In the late 1800s and early 1900s, railroads replaced horses as the main way of moving goods across long distances by land. People began to use tractors and other machines for farming and mining. Fewer draft horses were bred. The Clydesdale was in danger of disappearing.

Breeders in Scotland wanted to save this horse. They started the Clydesdale Horse Society in 1877. Its mission is to help the Clydesdale breed continue. It keeps records of all Clydesdale foals that are born. It also holds shows for Clydesdale horses.

Further Evidence

Read the article below. Does it give any new evidence to support Chapter Two?

All about Horses

abdocorelibrary.com/clydesdale

A Clydesdale should have a straight head and look strong.

CHAPTER 3

LIVING WITH THE CLYDESDALE

Clydesdale horses are known for their large size and strong build. They usually stand 16.2 to 18 hands tall. A hand is 4 inches (10 cm). Clydesdales weigh between 1,600 and 2,200 pounds (730 and 1,000 kg).

A Clydesdale's hooves can be the size of a dinner plate! The horses have long, silky hair called feathers on their lower legs. They lift their legs high when they move. They take long strides.

Clydesdales are often bay in color, which is reddish brown with a black mane and tail. They can also be black, gray, **chestnut**, or **roan**. Clydesdales usually have white markings on their faces and legs.

Pulling and Shows

Draft horses are not used as much for farm work today. Machines do these jobs now. But some people still use horses as a more natural way of farming.

Parts of a Harness

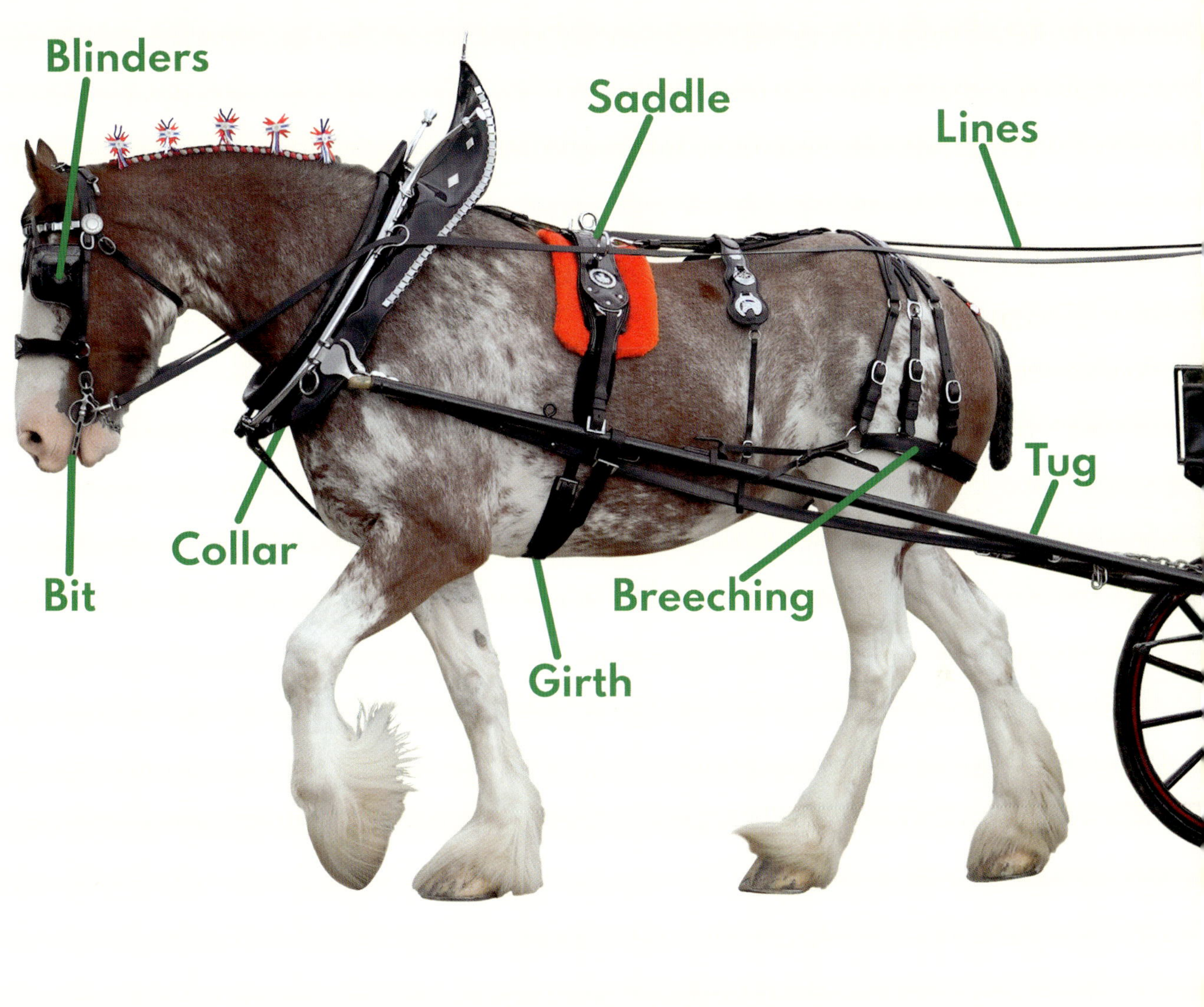

Clydesdales and other horses are hitched to vehicles such as sleds or carriages using a harness. It allows the horse to pull the vehicle's weight while the driver guides the speed and direction of the horse.

In halter class, a judge ranks Clydesdales based on how well they match the ideal look for the breed.

Clydesdales pull more than just farm equipment. Sometimes Clydesdales pull carriages for weddings and other special events. These horses may pull wagons for hay rides. Or they can pull sleighs in winter. Clydesdale owners often say their horses enjoy working and feeling useful.

The breed can compete in pulling contests. In hitch classes, teams of horses are driven with different types of carts and carriages. Clydesdales are often hitched in teams of two, four, or more. The world record for the biggest draft horse hitch is held by a team of 50 Clydesdale horses. They were driven for nearly 2 miles (3.2 km) at a town fair in Ontario, Canada.

Halter classes are another show Clydesdales compete in. A handler leads the horse. They show off the horse's looks and movement.

Saddle Up!

More people are realizing that Clydesdales can be great riding horses. Clydesdales compete in riding shows. In English classes, riders hold the reins with two hands. They show their horses using **gaits** called the walk, trot, and canter. In Western classes, people hold the reins in one hand. They show their horses at the walk, jog, and lope. English gaits are faster and cover more ground. Western gaits are slower to help a horse save energy.

Galloping Giants

There is a race in Devon, England, that is just for Clydesdales. The horses are ridden by professional **jockeys**. The race is a fundraiser for an air ambulance charity.

English classes, *pictured*, use smaller, lighter saddles than Western classes.

Clydesdales can make loving companions.

Clydesdales can also do dressage. In this sport, a horse and rider perform a pattern of movements called a test. Some tests ask a horse to collect, or shorten its stride. Others ask it to extend, or lengthen its stride. Although Clydesdales were not bred for this sport, many are quite good at it. Sometimes Clydesdales are crossed with Thoroughbreds to make strong, athletic riding horses.

Clydesdales and other draft breeds are a kind of living history. They are a reminder of how much people once relied on horsepower. And they continue to inspire with their beauty and strength.

Explore Online

Watch the video below. Does it give any new evidence to support Chapter Three?

Paw Classic: A Trip to a Clydesdale Farm

abdocorelibrary.com/clydesdale

BREED TRAITS

Powerful hindquarters

Large hooves